NATASHA GORDON

Nine Night is Natasha Gordon's first play as a writer. She won the
Charles Wintour Award for Most Promising Playwright at the
2018 Evening Standard Awards. As an actor, her work in theatre
includes *Red Velvet* at the Tricycle; *The Low Road* and *Clubland*
at the Royal Court; *Mules* and *The Exception and the Rule* at the
Young Vic; *Luce* at Southwark Playhouse; and *As You Like It* and
Cymbeline at the RSC. Film includes *Dough*. TV includes *Class*,
EastEnders, *Line of Duty*, *Danny and the Human Zoo*, *You, Me
and the Apocalypse*, *Secret Words* and *Law and Order: UK*.

Other Titles in this Series

Natasha Gordon

NINE NIGHT

NICK HERN BOOKS

London

www.nickhernbooks.co.uk

A Nick Hern Book

Nine Night first published in Great Britain in 2018 as a paperback original by Nick Hern Books Limited, The Glasshouse, 49a Goldhawk Road, London W12 8QP

Reprinted in this new edition in 2018

Nine Night copyright © 2018 Natasha Gordon

Natasha Gordon has asserted her right to be identified as the author of this work

Cover photography by Sorted
Design by National Theatre Graphic Design Studio

Designed and typeset by Nick Hern Books, London
Printed in Great Britain by Mimeo Ltd, Huntingdon, Cambridgeshire PE29 6XX

A CIP catalogue record for this book is available from the British Library

ISBN 978 1 84842 730 3

Nine Night was first performed in the Dorfman auditorium of the National Theatre, London, on 30 April 2018 (previews from 21 April). The cast was as follows:

ROBERT	Oliver Alvin-Wilson
LORRAINE	Franc Ashman
UNCLE VINCE	Ricky Fearon
TRUDY	Michelle Greenidge
SOPHIE	Hattie Ladbury
ANITA	Rebekah Murrell
AUNT MAGGIE	Cecilia Noble

Director	Roy Alexander Weise
Designer	Rajha Shakiry
Lighting Designer	Paule Constable
Sound Designer	George Dennis
Movement Director	Shelley Maxwell
Fight Director	Bret Yount
Company Voice Work	Rebecca Cuthbertson
Dialect Coach	Hazel Holder
Staff Director	Jade Lewis
Assistant to the Movement Director	Sarita Piotrowski

The play transferred to Trafalgar Studios, London, on 1 December 2018, with the following changes to the cast:

LORRAINE	Natasha Gordon
UNCLE VINCE	Karl Collins

Acknowledgements

This play was born from the support network of an incredible group of women.
Sisters, your belief in me has birthed a playwright.
Amelia Adrian, Michele Austin, Rakie Ayola,
Sharon Duncan-Brewster and Ashley Miller.
Thanks forever.

Many thanks to:
Rufus Norris
Ben Power

To the cast and creative team at the NT

To Katie Haines

To Ruby Gordon

To my family

For your support and encouragement, special thanks to:
Emily McLaughlin
Indhu Rubasingham
and especially to Dominic Cooke for making this happen.
I am eternally grateful.

Lastly, to Tom Anderson for absolutely everything.

N.G.

To Ella and Reuben

Characters

ANITA, *Lorraine's daughter, twenties, mixed race*
LORRAINE, *Gloria's daughter, mid-forties, black*
MAGGIE, *Gloria's cousin, seventies, black*
VINCE, *Maggie's husband, seventies, black*
ROBERT, *Gloria's son, early forties, black*
SOPHIE, *Robert's wife, mid-forties, white*
TRUDY, *Lorraine and Robert's half-sister, early fifties, black*

Note on Text

Where there is a / in the text, the next character starts speaking.

This text went to press before the end of rehearsals and so may differ slightly from the play as performed.

Scene One

Lights up on: a roomy seventies-style kitchen. The furniture is old-fashioned. Deco is typical of an elder West Indian. There is elaborate wallpaper that has been up since the 1970s, lots of house plants, pictures and relics of Jesus and the Virgin Mary on the walls, shelves full of ornaments and crocheted placemats. Around the room there are several headshots of a boy and girl taken together at school, throughout the years.

There are three doors in this room: one upstage-right slightly off-centre, one upstage-left and one downstage-left. The upstage-left door leads to the front room, the upstage-right door leads to the hallway, front door and rest of the house. The downstage-left door is the back door, leading to the garden. There is a sink and some cupboards downstage-right. There is also a table and chairs and a sofa.

We open on ANITA *at the kitchen sink making a pink powdered drink that looks a bit like milkshake. We watch her put three heaped teaspoons of powder into a mug.*

ANITA. Shit!

She pours water from the kettle into the mug. She lifts the mixture up with the spoon and allows it to fall back into the mug. She stirs it, then sniffs it.

Rank.

She is about to head up the stairs, through the door upstage-right, when she realises she has forgotten something. She goes back to the sink and starts rummaging through the drawers.

She checks the cupboards.

She walks to the bottom of the stairs and shouts.

Can't find the straws.

Beat.

Mum?

Beat.

Shall I just bring a teaspoon?

From upstairs we hear –

LORRAINE (*offstage*). Have you looked in the drawers?

ANITA. Yes.

LORRAINE (*offstage*). Have you checked in the cupboards?

ANITA. Yes.

LORRAINE (*offstage*). They were there yesterday.

ANITA. I know. I put them there.

LORRAINE (*offstage*). So, just bring a spoon, Anita.
A tablespoon. Teaspoons are fiddly.

The doorbell rings.

ANITA. Bloody hell.

Beat.

It rings again.

LORRAINE (*offstage*). Anita, the door?

ANITA. Yes, I know. I'm going – Answering doors, looking for
straws – Anything else?

ANITA *turns to go* – MAGGIE *and* VINCE *enter from
upstage-right.*

ANITA *jumps.*

Jesus Christ!

VINCE. De door left open.

ANITA. Was it?

MAGGIE. Yuh mad? Any and anybody could jus' walk in.

ANITA. Tell me about it.

MAGGIE. Be careful, not carefree.

ANITA. The lock keeps sticking. Uncle Robert's been promising to fix it. Does Mum know you're coming?

MAGGIE. Me ring ha dis morning. Where yu grandmadda?

ANITA. She's upstairs.

VINCE. It turn bad-bad?

ANITA.... Yes.

MAGGIE. But, is just the udda day me a sit down and a chat wid ha, good-good. It's like she just give up after me leave.

ANITA. No, I don't think so. / It's just taken its toll.

MAGGIE. Lord have mercy. (*To* VINCE.) Me tell yuh. She shoulda drink de bush tea whe me tell ha fi drink. You know how many people life dat ting save in Jamaica?

Beat.

ANITA. Shall I take your coats?

VINCE. Tank yuh, dawta.

VINCE *takes off his coat and hands it to* ANITA.

MAGGIE. Dees doctor inna dis country, don't know dem head from dem foot! All now, dem a look right, dem a look left fi find cure for dis cancer business. If she, Gloria, was in Jamaica, dem woulda stop dis nonsense long time!

ANITA. Your coat, Auntie Maggie?

MAGGIE. No, tank you. It might be summer dem call dis, but I feeling de cold. Where yuh madda?

ANITA. Upstairs, with Grandma.

MAGGIE. Tell her fi come down.

VINCE *and* MAGGIE *sit down.*

ANITA *walks to the bottom of the stairs and calls out.*

ANITA. Uncle Vince and Auntie Maggie are here.

Beat.

She'll be down in a minute.

MAGGIE *eyes* ANITA.

MAGGIE. Yuh know, back home in Jamaica, me have dis cousin. Rosemary. She big suh, like yuh grandmadda. Last year, she phone me. Bawling – di doctor seh she have diabetes and him ready fi chop off she foot. Now me tell ha, 'Rosemary, save yuh eye water, nuh badda cry', and I tell ha fi mek dat same bush tea whe me advise yuh grandmadda to tek. Rosemary boil up di leaf dem; chamomile, cerasee, duppy-gun and donkey-weed. As God is my witness, mek Him strike me down if one word I speak is a lie! You tell me where dat diabetes is now? Ehh?

Beat.

It gawn!

ANITA. Yeah. Or maybe they misdiagnosed it. Speaking of tea, would you like a drink?

VINCE. Yu have anyting harder dan tea?

ANITA. I'll have a look. Auntie Maggie?

MAGGIE. Which kinda tea yuh 'ave?

ANITA. Dunno. Builder's? Peppermint?

MAGGIE. Dat's all?

ANITA. It's not my kitchen, so –

MAGGIE. Just give me some wata – Not from de tap, if yuh please.

ANITA. I'll see what I can find.

ANITA *exits upstage-right, taking* VINCE*'s coat.*

VINCE *and* MAGGIE *sit in silence.* MAGGIE *sniffs the air.*

MAGGIE (*whisper*). You smell it, Vin?

VINCE. Smell wha?

Beat.

MAGGIE. She travelling, alright.

ANITA *returns without the coats carrying an open bottle of brandy and a small can of Coke*.

ANITA. You're in luck, Uncle Vince. I found some brandy.

VINCE. God bless yu.

ANITA. Can of Coke to go with it?

VINCE. Nah sah, dat's a woman's drink. I tek it as it comes.

ANITA *pours brandy for* VINCE *then heads to the fridge to get water for* MAGGIE.

MAGGIE. Nah badda start pon dat drink business and turn fool pon me yuh hear? Me nah carry yuh home tonight.

VINCE. Calm yuh nerves, woman.

ANITA. How did you get here?

VINCE. Yvette drop we off.

ANITA. Did she?

MAGGIE. In she new brand car.

ANITA. Nice.

MAGGIE. It is. Very, very nice indeed.

ANITA. She didn't fancy popping in?

MAGGIE. Yuh know how she always busy. We lucky that she even in the country this week to give us a lift.

ANITA. The job's working out, is it?

MAGGIE. She living de life, my dear. Last week she travel business class to New York. Next week she travelling premium class to – to… Whe she a go, Vince? India?

VINCE. Indonesia.

MAGGIE. Indonesia. She spreading she talent across de whole world.

ANITA *gives them their drinks.* VINCE *take a sip of brandy.*

ANITA. Yeah. I don't know how she does it, balancing all those drinks and dinners midair. She always did love make-up, I suppose.

Beat.

MAGGIE *watches* ANITA.

MAGGIE. Yu turn Rasta now?

ANITA. Sorry?

MAGGIE. Yu new hair style.

ANITA. It's an experiment actually.

MAGGIE. Experiment?

ANITA. Nathan and I are challenging the subtleties of discrimination – how long can we go without combing our hair before we feel –

MAGGIE. Headlice?

ANITA. Pressure to conform.

VINCE. Dat sound interesting.

ANITA. People are still trying to define us by our roots, Uncle V, literally. People wanna check out their politics before they're checking my hair.

MAGGIE. How is Nathan? Him still not working?

ANITA. He's finishing his PhD.

MAGGIE. / Still?

VINCE. How de baby?

ANITA. Rosa? She's fine, thank you.

MAGGIE. How old she is now?

ANITA. Nine months.

VINCE. She gettin' big.

ANITA. Yeah, she's growing fast.

MAGGIE. She a good baby?

ANITA. She's a great baby.

MAGGIE. She sleep good?

ANITA. Yep.

MAGGIE. Right through the night?

ANITA. Yep.

MAGGIE. She like she food?

VINCE. Jesus Christ! Is why yu a interrogate de chile?

MAGGIE. Is not an interrogation fi ask a simple question –

ANITA. She's mostly on breast milk / and –

MAGGIE. Breast milk?

ANITA. Yep.

MAGGIE. At nine months?

ANITA. The antibodies in –

MAGGIE. Poor ting must be longing fi a piece of chicken.

> MAGGIE *takes a glug of water and chokes.*

ANITA. Are you alright? Sorry, I didn't get a chance to say, it's sparkling. I hate that, when things get up your nose. I better take Grandma's drink up.

> ANITA *exits, upstage-right.*

MAGGIE (*speaking quietly*). I wonder if dem ring Trudy yet?

> *Beat.*

> I bet dem nuh ring ha.

> *Beat.*

Remind me, fi ring ha dis evening.

Beat.

A nuh yuh me a talk to?

VINCE. Lard, Maggie. Lef people business alone nuh, man.

MAGGIE *points to a picture of Gloria up on the wall.*

MAGGIE. Pssst…

VINCE. Wha?

MAGGIE. Me bet a dat one dem a go use. Fi di coffin.

She gets up and throws her glass of water away. She waters a dry-looking plant.

She picks up an ornament of a glass fish.

Me did 'ave one like dis, remember?

VINCE. Put dat down, Maggie.

MAGGIE *jumps as* LORRAINE *enters with the powdery drink that* ANITA *made.* LORRAINE *clocks* MAGGIE *with the fish.* VINCE *stands up.* MAGGIE *puts the fish back.*

LORRAINE. Hello, Auntie Maggie, Uncle Vince.

They greet each other with hugs and kisses.

Nice of you to visit, you didn't / say –

MAGGIE. Me couldn't believe when me ring dis morning and yuh tell me seh Gloria gawn down suh.

VINCE. We can see ha?

LORRAINE. It's a bit awkward. She's only just got back off to sleep.

MAGGIE. After me travel all dis way on me bad hip?

LORRAINE. I wasn't expecting you. / If you had said –

VINCE. We understand.

LORRAINE. She's had a rough night – maybe / tomorrow –

MAGGIE. Last night me dream seh, me see ha, flying high pon a white dove. She land right in front of me, stretch out she neck like ostrich and seh 'Maggie, me beg yuh read me Psalm 23.' So, me tell Vincent, even if me haffi cripple wid pain dis marning, dis day can't pass and me nah see Gloria, me good-good cousin.

Beat.

LORRAINE. You'll need to be really quiet.

MAGGIE *goes to her bag and rummages for her Bible.*

VINCE. How long?

LORRAINE. Weeks… Days.

VINCE. Jesus-Christ-Almighty-Farda-God-in-Heaven.

MAGGIE. Stop bawl down de Lard name. 'Im busy enough. Come, mek we go and see.

MAGGIE *and* VINCE *head up the stairs.*

LORRAINE *goes to the sink and throws away the powdery drink. She takes her phone out of her pocket and dials.*

LORRAINE. Robert. It's me. Again. Call me back.

Scene Two

ROBERT *and* ANITA *are at opposite sides of the table.*
SOPHIE *is standing.* LORRAINE *is chopping vegetables.*
There's a vase of big sunflowers on the table.

ROBERT. Is she ever gonna wake up?

ANITA. What's the time?

SOPHIE. Half past two.

ANITA. You need to put a permit in your car, Mum.

ROBERT. Can anyone smell that?

SOPHIE. Smells delicious.

ROBERT. Not the food – Kinda dank smell.

Beat.

She hasn't budged. I've been here since ten.

ANITA. Eleven.

ROBERT. What?

ANITA. You got here at eleven.

ROBERT *looks at* ANITA.

ROBERT. What's that thing in her arm?

Beat.

Lorraine?

ANITA. It's a subcutaneous needle.

ROBERT. A what?

ANITA. It automatically administers the morphine.

ROBERT. So, that's why she's knocked out – Lorraine?

ANITA. It doesn't knock her out, it keeps her comfortable.

ROBERT. It's not right. She can't move, can't / talk.

ANITA. She smiled this morning when we were changing her.

SOPHIE. Showing off those fantastic teeth, no doubt.

ROBERT. Why are you changing her?

ANITA. As oppose to?

ROBERT. The nurses.

ANITA. What / nurses?

SOPHIE. Is it me, or is it unbearably hot?

ROBERT. They're qualified professionals, carrying out proper procedures.

SOPHIE. Anybody mind if I open the window?

SOPHIE *gets up*.

ROBERT. There's a proper way to do things. What if you drop her?

SOPHIE *opens the window*.

ANITA. You want us to leave her to lie in her piss while we wait for qualified professionals to carry out / proper procedures.

ROBERT. When I left on Monday she was compos mentis.

SOPHIE. Can I help with anything, Lorraine?

ROBERT. She was lively, sitting up, cracking joke.

ANITA. No, she wasn't.

ROBERT. Yes, she was.

SOPHIE. Why don't I chop the rest of the veg.

ROBERT. You weren't even here.

ANITA. Yes, / I was.

ROBERT. Not / at the same time as me you weren't.

SOPHIE. I must have told you, I was the fastest chopper in Home Economics. I could dice a seven-inch carrot in under twenty seconds. Still can. So, happy to / help if –

LORRAINE. Fuck!

SOPHIE. Oh God, did you slice through?

LORRAINE. Fuck!

ANITA. Is it deep?

SOPHIE. I'll mop up vomit, but I cannot stand the sight of blood.

LORRAINE. It's not my finger. It's the chilli.

ANITA. Chilli?

SOPHIE. Ah. In the eye. I did that once. Hurts much more than it should. Here, let me –

LORRAINE. I'm fine. Can everyone just…

    LORRAINE *goes to the sink.*

    Silence.

SOPHIE. Any news, Anita?

ANITA. Not really.

SOPHIE. Oh. Well, I suppose Rosa takes up all your time these days. We'd babysit, you know, / if you wanted to go out – give the establishment what for. Or just have a night out.

ROBERT. Would we?

ANITA. Thanks.

SOPHIE. I talk about you and Nathan all the time. To my students. I hold you up as an example. Your responsibilities haven't held you back – a new wave of radicals –

ANITA. We're not radicals.

SOPHIE. No, I wasn't / implying –

ANITA. Self-empowerment is not radicalism. That's exactly the kind of rhetoric the media use. Throw around buzzwords as a means to distract while their government drags us deeper into oppression.

SOPHIE. I was referring to your chutzpah, really.

ROBERT. I bet they love you at baby groups.

ANITA. I don't do / baby groups.

SOPHIE. How's the eye, Lorraine?

Beat.

ROBERT. Mum doesn't eat chilli.

LORRAINE. It's not chilli, it's a soup. I saw a recipe on a forum
– foods that fight cancer. Thought it might be worth a try.

Beat.

SOPHIE. Any news on Trudy?

ROBERT. What?

SOPHIE. Just wondering if there's been an update.

Beat.

I think it would be a shame if she didn't come over. Do you
think she realises – ?

ROBERT. Of course she realises.

SOPHIE. Yes, but has she taken in, how / quickly –

ROBERT. She's not interested.

SOPHIE. Have you actually explained to her – ?

ROBERT. What difference would it make?

SOPHIE. It's an opportunity for her to say goodbye to her
mother.

ROBERT. It's an opportunity for her to get her foot on British
soil, suffocate some poor bastard with her pum-pum / and
start seeking a British passport and whatever else she can get
her hands on.

ANITA. Pum-pum, are you for real?

SOPHIE. She's your sister.

ROBERT. Half-sister.

SOPHIE. I don't mind phoning her –

LORRAINE. No, thank you, actually, Sophie –

SOPHIE. Just imagine if she did make the trip from Jamaica, the difference it could make to Gloria.

ROBERT. How's she going to notice when she's practically in a coma.

SOPHIE. She can still hear us, smell us even. For all you know she could be lying there / waiting –

ROBERT. She's not.

SOPHIE. You don't know that –

ROBERT. I know my mum. She's not lying there waiting for Trudy. She stopped waiting for that woman years ago.

LORRAINE *looks out the window.*

ANITA. She's not in a coma. She knows exactly what's going on.

LORRAINE. Is that rain? It's bloody raining. Anita, get the basket.

ANITA *goes to get the basket.*

ROBERT *kisses his teeth and gets up to go.*

Hold up – where are you going?

ROBERT. What d'you mean, where am I going? – to see if she's woken up.

ANITA. Where is it, Mum?

LORRAINE. You'll have to wait ten minutes.

ROBERT. Wait / for what?

ANITA. Mum?

SOPHIE. Under the sink, Anita.

LORRAINE. It's time for her to have her Complan. Anita, get one ready.

ROBERT. Her what?

LORRAINE. It's better she drinks it before she has visitors.

ROBERT. Visitors? Are you taking the –

SOPHIE. I'll make the Complan –

LORRAINE. No thank you, actually, Sophie – She hasn't seen you for a couple of a days. She'll get distracted and she won't swallow properly.

ANITA. You can get the washing.

ANITA hands SOPHIE the basket.

ROBERT. What are you carrying on with, Lorraine?

LORRAINE. You said yourself – there's a proper way to do things.

ROBERT. I've been waiting since ten o'clock.

ANITA. Eleven.

ROBERT. Who's talking to you?

SOPHIE exits downstage-left with the basket.

LORRAINE. It'd be a shame wouldn't it; to fight the cancer, but die from choking.

ANITA. Mum, she can't fight the –

LORRAINE. No. But, I'm not just going to write her off, am I?

ROBERT sits back down. They sit in silence as LORRAINE chops and ANITA prepares a Complan.

What was that?

ANITA. What was what?

Slight beat.

Mum?

LORRAINE. Is it ready?

ANITA. Yes.

ANITA takes a spoon out of the drawer.

LORRAINE takes the glass and the spoon from ANITA. She throws the spoon in the sink.

LORRAINE. The straws are next to the fridge.

> LORRAINE *exits upstage-right*. ANITA *gets a straw and follows*.

> SOPHIE *re-enters*.

> *She puts the washing down.*

> *Silence.*

SOPHIE. Funny weather. The sun's back out.

> *Beat.*

> Beautiful flowers. Fresh. Where did you get them?

> *Beat.*

> Sunflowers were our first success. Do you remember? In the garden of the old flat. You used to look good in pair of wellies. Funny to think now, but we got quite into that garden, before we gave up and covered everything in evergreens.

> ROBERT *gets up*.

ROBERT. Why bring up Trudy?

SOPHIE. Look – I know you don't see eye to eye, but I thought if I offered to call, it might help.

ROBERT. Help? Can't you see Miss Seacole's driving this ship. There ain't no room for Florence.

SOPHIE. We're not at war, Robert.

ROBERT. Don't come running to me when she flings your arse overboard.

SOPHIE. Probably not your best analogy – given I'm the only one here that can actually swim.

ROBERT. What?

SOPHIE. Look, Robert –

ROBERT. You know, for a music teacher, you've got a shit sense of timing.

SOPHIE. You're absolutely right. There is something in the air – it's insufferable.

LORRAINE *appears at the doorway with the Complan.*

LORRAINE. You can go up.

ROBERT. She didn't even drink it? After all that?

ROBERT *exits upstage-right.*

LORRAINE *empties the Complan down the sink.*

SOPHIE. I bet she's saving her appetite for the soup.

LORRAINE *picks up her jacket and makes for the upstage-right door.*

LORRAINE. I'll be back in a bit.

SOPHIE. Shall I turn the soup off?

LORRAINE. No… Yes.

SOPHIE. Permit?

LORRAINE *exits, without the permit.*

SOPHIE *watches her go.*

SOPHIE *alone.*

She rubs her stomach.

She lifts up her top, puts her hands on her belly and closes her eyes.

She sits for a few moments in silence.

We hear footsteps coming down the stairs very fast. SOPHIE *opens her eyes and quickly drops her top.*

ANITA (*offstage*). Mum!

ANITA *enters.*

Where's Mum?

SOPHIE. I –

ANITA. Where is she, Sophie?!

SOPHIE. I don't know. She / said –

ANITA. Grandma, her breathing. She's –

SOPHIE. Oh, God.

ROBERT (*offstage*). No, no / no, no, no, no, no, no, no, no, no, no, no, no, no, no, no…

ANITA. Find her, / Sophie.

SOPHIE. Oh, God – she can't have got far –

ANITA. Just get her. Get her quickly.

> ANITA *exits upstage-right – heading back upstairs.*

> SOPHIE *exits upstage-right – heading for the front door.*

Scene Three

In the kitchen. There are lots of bouquets of flowers. The table is full of bottles of wine, rum, beer and finger snacks. LORRAINE *is holding onto the back of a chair.* ANITA *stands by the upstage-left door, holding a tray. 'Dollar Wine' by Colin Lucas is blaring from the front room.*

We are into the third night of the Nine.

LORRAINE *and* ANITA *are still as the music plays for a few beats.*

ANITA *moves from the door.*

ANITA. How many more nights?

> Her next door's already complained. Can't Uncle Robert hold this shindig at his house? They've got a big enough gaff.
> You're done in. Nathan's taken Rosa home early, cos Auntie Maggie keeps trying to sneak chicken bones in her mouth.

I don't know who half of them are in there. They don't know me, yet seem to think my name's 'Waitress'. And what's-her-name with the bright purple weave – Miss Stacey – looks more like she's going to Carnival than coming for a wake. Why don't you just stay at home tomorrow night? Let them congregate in a pub if they wanna drink and make noise.

Beat.

Mum?

LORRAINE. Three things you don't mess with when it comes to Jamaicans, Anita. Their money, their food and their traditions. You, of all people, should understand that. Nine nights of mourning. They're paying their respects.

ANITA. They're nyaming out our food and drink. Right, that music's going down.

ANITA *exits upstage-left.*

LORRAINE *pours herself a drink.*

The music becomes quieter.

MAGGIE *enters from upstage-right.*

MAGGIE. Vincent is in 'ere?

LORRAINE. No.

MAGGIE. Yuh see 'im?

LORRAINE. No.

MAGGIE. Suh, wheh dat man gawn?

LORRAINE. ...I don't know.

MAGGIE. Me tell him already dat we not stopping long. Me wan fi get home fi watch *EastEnder*. Big tings are gawn in de Queen Vic tonight!

MAGGIE *exits upstage-right.*

ANITA *enters from upstage-left.*

ANITA. Spoons. We need serving spoons.

ANITA *goes to the cutlery drawer.*

Feisty Miss Stacey just cussed off Sophie for dipping her hands into the peanut bowl – 'Yuh hand clean?' And she's one to talk. Her hands have been all over Uncle Vince. Twice she's pulled down her top to show him a scar on her shoulder, 'Left over from me operation.'

She'll need another one if Maggie catches her.

SOPHIE *enters from upstage-left.*

You alright?

SOPHIE. No harm done.

ANITA *exits upstage-left with spoons.*

Right. Time I was heading off.

Slight beat.

Lorraine?

LORRAINE. Yeah. Sorry about the peanuts. She's –

SOPHIE. No, no, my fault. I forgot myself – I probably shouldn't be eating them any way – well – not that I shouldn't be – it's just – it's – goodness, I had an early start this morning, I think it's finally catching up with me… It's been lovely tonight. Really, it has. Not sure I can make it tomorrow, end-of-term reports to write –

LORRAINE. You don't have to –

SOPHIE. No, I'd like to attend each night. For Gloria. I hope you liked the cake. I didn't know what else to bring. It was lively tonight… With the music. I didn't think they'd be dancing. Is that usual?

Beat.

Lorraine?

LORRAINE. Those pills you gave me?

SOPHIE. Brilliant, aren't they?

LORRAINE. They're for depression. I'm not depressed.

SOPHIE. No. But –

LORRAINE. Are you alright? I / mean –

SOPHIE. They help me to sleep. The one thing I've never been any good at. Still, it's improved since I started yoga – it's – I – I – Sorry –

LORRAINE. It's alright.

SOPHIE. I thought the pills might help you to – but – you're – God, sorry, Lorraine. You're the one that should be –

LORRAINE. You're allowed to be upset.

SOPHIE. I miss her. She was one of the kindest people I ever – I'm really sorry.

LORRAINE. You don't need to apologise.

SOPHIE. I don't know how you're managing it, but you're doing brilliantly. All of this company must be of comfort. It – it was nothing like this when my dad passed away. I think a neighbour brought food round for the first few days, but it felt like people were avoiding us mostly. Some people couldn't even look me in the eye. Funny, how some people don't know what to say, whereas others say too much.

LORRAINE. Yeah.

SOPHIE. Oh, God. Sorry – am I – ?

LORRAINE. No.

SOPHIE. Dad passed away in the middle of the night and my mother decided it'd be better if I got a full night's sleep rather than wake me. My sister was there. I think about that less now. You nursed Gloria till the very end. That's all that really matters.

Beat.

LORRAINE. I've been dipping into this book, about the different layers of grief. Apparently, your loved ones only appear to you in a dream once your subconscious has processed the loss.

SOPHIE. Funny. Robert dreamt about her last night.

LORRAINE. Did he?

SOPHIE. Oh, I think it was very brief... It was months before I dreamt about Dad. I sat up for three nights after he died; in the kitchen, waiting, cross-legged, staring at a candle.

LORRAINE. In the kitchen?

SOPHIE. Well, you wouldn't want a ghost to appear in your bedroom – that would be spooky.

LORRAINE. So did he? Appear?

SOPHIE. No, but he did send a sign. On the day of his funeral. We were driving to the crematorium and a white feather flew in from the window and landed on my shoulder. He was mad for birds.

Slight beat.

LORRAINE. I hope I get a sign.

SOPHIE. You're bound to.

LORRAINE. Not a feather though – too subtle. More like a frying pan / in the back of my head.

SOPHIE. In the back of your head.

/ Ha!

LORRAINE. Ha!

Beat.

Why shouldn't you be eating peanuts?

SOPHIE. Sorry?

LORRAINE. You / said –

SOPHIE. Oh, they're fattening, aren't they?

LORRAINE. Peanuts?

MAGGIE *re-enters from upstage-right.*

MAGGIE. Yuh find him?

SOPHIE. Who?

MAGGIE. Vincent.

LORRAINE. Have you checked outside, Auntie Maggie?

MAGGIE. No.

LORRAINE. Well, he's probably out there.

MAGGIE. I don't know.

SOPHIE. I'll check on my way out?

MAGGIE. Yuh leaving already?

SOPHIE. Early start tomorrow.

MAGGIE. Me too. Lorraine, please – beg yuh go look fi him. Di hip giving me problem. Tell 'im me ready.

SOPHIE. I'll go –

MAGGIE. Lorraine will do it.

LORRAINE *exits upstage-right.*

What a beautiful evening. Word really travel pon mout. Me never even notice de time fly so quick. Yvette was going to pick we up dis evening, but she haffi work. Suh, we haffi brace de cold, cold, freezing cold.

SOPHIE.… Would you like a lift?

MAGGIE. I like to use my Freedom Pass. It's de only decent ting me get from dis teefing Government, an' me intend to get full use outta it before me dead. Look pon Gloria. She get good use outta it before God call she. De whole of North London she travel with it. The 41 bus. The 444. The 43. The 236 –

SOPHIE. Yes, she certainly was one for getting around.

MAGGIE (*lets out a dirty laugh*). You can say dat again.

SOPHIE. Sorry?

MAGGIE. Wheh you live again?

SOPHIE. Hackney.

MAGGIE. Yuh still live round dem side? Wheh dem a stab up people like it a competition? Yuh good.

SOPHIE. You really wouldn't recognise it now.

MAGGIE. Well, yuh can live de risky life. Yuh nuh 'ave any pickney fi tink bout. Is where Yvette used to live. But, she move, with the help of Jesus. She have a very nice flat in Muswell Hill now… Wid seh fiancé.

SOPHIE. Goodness. Yvette's getting married?

MAGGIE. Well, I'm not suppose to tell anybody really. (*Whispers*.) Between me and yuh.

SOPHIE. Congratulations! That's great news.

MAGGIE. It's wonderful news. Shame Gloria won't be here to see it. Gloria love a wedding. And yuh know what happen after marriage? / Finally, I will be a grandmadda. And dat pickney will have tall, Indian-like hair. Like my side of de family. Gloria always admire my Yvette hair. Lorraine could shave off she head and mek a back scrub – Yuh enjoy dis evening?

SOPHIE. Divorce?

I'm not sure 'enjoy' is the right word.

MAGGIE. How yuh mean? Is not fi yuh. Is fi Gloria.

ROBERT *enters from upstage-right, carting a bottle of rum.*

ROBERT. Evening all.

MAGGIE. Ah! De prodigal son return! Where yuh been hiding?

ROBERT. Good to see you, Auntie M.

She gives ROBERT *a warm hug.*

MAGGIE. Me sorry for yuh loss, darling. But, such is life. The Lard giveth, suh him haffi tek wheh.

ROBERT. Yep.

MAGGIE. Yuh put on weight. Wifey must be looking after yuh good.

ROBERT. And you're looking well.

MAGGIE. Oh, yuh know, with the help of Jesus.

LORRAINE *re-enters from upstage-right*.

LORRAINE. He is outside, Auntie Maggie.

MAGGIE. Wheh him a do out deh?

LORRAINE (*to* ROBERT). Decided to put in an appearance? (*To* MAGGIE.) Chatting to George.

MAGGIE. Mad George?

ROBERT *gets a message through on his phone. He replies*.

LORRAINE (*to* MAGGIE). George Carter.

MAGGIE. Him mad, yes. I bet dem a chat pure fart.

LORRAINE. They were talking about you actually.

MAGGIE. Me?

LORRAINE. Yeah. Some dance you went to in the sixties. Uncle Vince says he arrived at that party with Mum / but –

MAGGIE. Sophie, come on –

LORRAINE. He left the party with you.

MAGGIE. Time fi tek we 'ome –

LORRAINE. He's calling it an ambush.

MAGGIE. Blasted man, yuh wait…

MAGGIE *storms out*.

SOPHIE. I think he might be in trouble.

MAGGIE (*offstage*). Sophie!

LORRAINE. He's too drunk to notice – you might be though.

SOPHIE. Wish me luck.

ROBERT *puts the rum on the table.*

See you later, darling.

ROBERT. Yeah.

Beat.

SOPHIE. Night, Lorraine.

LORRAINE. Night. And thanks.

SOPHIE. Any time.

SOPHIE *exits.*

LORRAINE *watches* ROBERT *pour himself a drink.*

ROBERT. Thanks for what?

LORRAINE. She made a lovely cake.

Beat.

ROBERT. Is it busy in there?

LORRAINE. Not as busy as it was. People have been asking for you.

ROBERT. Like who?

LORRAINE. Show yer face and you'll find out.

Slight beat.

ROBERT. There's no rush. Chris sends his condolences, by the way.

LORRAINE. When does he get back from Hong Kong?

ROBERT. Not for a bit.

LORRAINE. So he's not coming to the funeral?

ROBERT. He can't.

LORRAINE. How many dinners has he eaten in this kitchen?

ROBERT. It's a stressful time, alright? He can't just drop everything.

LORRAINE. Peas in a pod.

ROBERT. Sorry?

LORRAINE. You and Chris.

ROBERT. You make patties, Lorraine. We make bread.

LORRAINE. What's that supposed to mean?

ROBERT. Don't worry about it.

ROBERT *picks at the snacks.*

LORRAINE. How are you sleeping?

ROBERT. Not great.

LORRAINE. Sophie said you dreamt about Mum.

ROBERT. Did she?

LORRAINE. What was she doing?

ROBERT. What?

LORRAINE. In the dream.

ROBERT. I don't know.

LORRAINE. How can you not know?

ROBERT. I can't remember.

LORRAINE. You must remember. You told Sophie.

ROBERT. I didn't tell Sophie anything. She heard me talking in my sleep.

LORRAINE. What did you say?

ROBERT. Lorraine – It's been the longest day. I just told you, I can't remember –

LORRAINE. Was she well? Did she –

ROBERT. We need to talk, Lorraine.

LORRAINE. Talk? Talk about what? –

ANITA *bursts in from upstage-left.*

ANITA. That's it. I'm gone. If I stay in that room a minute longer, it'll be more than Grandma that needs burying.

ANITA *starts to gather her things together.*

ROBERT. So what? You're not going to say anything?

LORRAINE. Say anything about what?

ROBERT. It's not the time to be cracking jokes.

ANITA. Who's joking? I'm going home to my baby, before I commit murder.

ROBERT. Everything for you is joke, innit? You should've skipped uni and gone to clown school –

LORRAINE. Robert – Don't rise, Anita.

ROBERT. I'm serious. Do you know how much money them mans make at Covent Garden juggling balls on a unicycle? You could actually pay your way instead of relying on your mum to bring you, your daughter and your man out of penury.

LORRAINE. Oh, / God –

ANITA. Remember that time when I was two and I pissed in your shoe –

LORRAINE. No, Anita. No.

ANITA. It wasn't because I didn't know any better. It was because of your shit taste in shoes –

ROBERT. See, this is what happens when you raise them without a father, / they lack breeding. You shouldn't even let her loose in there. She doesn't know how to speak to big people.

ANITA. Here we go same old, old, lame – at least I turn up.

I'm twenty-three!

ROBERT. I couldn't care if you were three hundred and five!

ANITA. Three hundred and five?

LORRAINE. Both / of you, stop it, now.

ANITA. That doesn't even make any sense! What's my name –
Methuselah, from the Bible?

ROBERT. Maybe if you studied the Bible more closely, you'd
have come home with a degree, instead of a baby.

ANITA. I came home with both – two things you can't buy
on Amex.

ROBERT. I buy whatever I like. I'm not interested in children,
or dressing up like Harry Potter for the day prancing around
in a gown, like a prick!

LORRAINE. You two really believe she's gone. That's why it's
alright for you to come in here, raise your voice and sharpen
your teeth. But this is still her house and she's still in it. Next
time you come, hang your bad-mindedness by the door. Or
don't bother coming at all… And, Anita, this isn't the place
to protest. Turn up tomorrow looking like Krusty the Clown,
and you'll leave looking like Ghandi.

LORRAINE *exits upstage-left.*

Scene Four

The middle of the same night. LORRAINE *sits in the kitchen,
cross-legged on the floor, staring at a candle.*

Scene Five

Night Four.

LORRAINE, ROBERT *and* VINCE *in the kitchen.*
LORRAINE *puts together bowls of finger snacks and drinks.*
She places them on a tray. ROBERT *and* VINCE *are at the*
table, mid-conversation.

VINCE. Stop it. Me belly a go bust!

ROBERT. Lorraine was there.

VINCE. Gloria was vex!

ROBERT. She was so adamant.

VINCE. She ring me cussing that marning.

ROBERT. I said, 'Mum, it's a bank – Are you sure the cashier
    short-changed you?'

VINCE. 'Dat woman teef me twenty pound!'

ROBERT. The commotion with the bank manager the next day –

VINCE. 'I'm sorry, Mrs Green, but we checked Cassandra's /
    till' –

ROBERT. Cassandra! That's it!

VINCE. 'It was perfectly balanced.'

ROBERT. Do the rest, Uncle V. I can't –

VINCE. 'Well, yuh can tell Cassandra; me twenty pound, whe
    she teef, me hope she tek it, buy food, it run she belly and
    she shit fi de whole week!'

    ROBERT *and* VINCE *crack up.*

ROBERT. The look on his face.

    LORRAINE *picks up the tray and exits upstage-left.*

    VINCE *refills their glasses. He raises his in the air.*

VINCE. Gloria.

    ROBERT *raises his glass.*

ROBERT. Mum.

They tip some rum onto the floor – a libation to Gloria – chink glasses and drink.

VINCE. Travel in peace.

Beat.

ROBERT. You were good to her, Uncle V. Good to us. You gave her strength, you know? Like Popeye drinking spinach. Remember the days you'd pick me up from school. In your Rover V8?

VINCE. Dat car did hold de road good. Best vehicle me ever 'ave.

ROBERT. The look on those kids' faces, like, 'Raa – where'd they get the money for that?'… And that Christmas, when you drove round to pick us up in it. The day Alvin walked out. I tried to lock myself in my room. Didn't want to see anybody. Mum near brock down the door.

VINCE. She used to seh, 'Shake off yuh dust; rise up – Isaiah 52.' As long as I know Gloria, nuttin ever keep she down fi long, and I see ha wrestle some real hardship.

ROBERT. It was you who talked me round though. In the absence of a father, we had you, and God. The other mums would shout, 'Wait till your father gets home.' Whereas Mum would say, 'When yuh get to Heaven, yuh see, God will deal wid yuh.' I was never sure if that was an incentive to behave or not.

VINCE. You farda wasn't a monster, Robert.

ROBERT. His name's Alvin, Uncle V.

Slight beat.

When I was a kid, I'd watch a black man walking down the street with his kids. I'd look at the kids and think, 'Are you gonna be one of the lucky ones? Or is he gonna fuck you up too?'… Yvette was one of the lucky ones, Uncle V.

VINCE. What about, Anita?

ROBERT. What about her?

VINCE. That farda she 'ave? Wid dem steely blue eye, as 'im look pon you, yuh blood freeze over. Anita wasn't lucky.

ROBERT. What? With all those summer holidays she gets to spend with him in the South of France. Most youth I know, Uncle V, ain't got money to top up their bus fare. All Anita's got to worry about is topping up her tan.

VINCE. She 'ave a small baby.

ROBERT. Whose fault is that?

Beat.

Yuh and I are quite similar, though.

VINCE. Yuh tink suh?

ROBERT. Yeah. We've both done well. Despite the odds.

VINCE. Well, yuh haffi elevate yuh self.

ROBERT. You took that to another level – the RAF.

VINCE. Fe a short while –

ROBERT. Your own garage –

VINCE. Fe over thirty years.

ROBERT. Did you give her money, Uncle V?

VINCE. Wha?

ROBERT. Mum. To keep the house.

VINCE....

ROBERT. It's alright. She didn't tell me. I worked it out.

VINCE. Look, Robert –

ROBERT. Maggie doesn't know, does she?

VINCE....No. And dat's de way it will stay.

ROBERT. How much?

VINCE. Robert –

ROBERT. Don't worry. I'm not going to say anything. How much?

VINCE. Dat's between / me and –

ROBERT. I'm gonna pay you back.

VINCE. Pay me back?

ROBERT. It's the least / I can –

VINCE. No, Robert, dat's not / what –

ROBERT. It's what she would want, Uncle V.

VINCE. Is trouble yuh a look, Robert?

ROBERT. She's sending me omens.

VINCE. How yuh mean?

ROBERT. Look, you know how Chris – business-partner Chris – has been back and forth to Hong Kong? Now get this, and I'm not a man big into dreams and dem tings, but the other night I dreamt she was calling me. I could hear her voice, but couldn't find her. I ran downstairs into the kitchen and Alvin was standing there staring at me. Mum came up behind him, carrying this big-arse machete. Just as I shouted, 'Mum, don't!', she split his head in two / and bare ten-, twenty- and all fifty-pound notes splattered across the room – I woke up drenched.

VINCE. Wha?

Serious ting.

ROBERT. Serious – it's a sign.

VINCE. She split 'im head inna two?

ROBERT. Like a melon –

VINCE. Jeeezzzz…

ROBERT. The business is gonna be big, Uncle V. I'm stepping it up.

VINCE. Fi real.

ROBERT. Come in on it.

VINCE. Wha?

Beat.

ROBERT. I've seen mans make thirty grand in less than an hour.

Beat.

The more you put in the bigger the margin.

Beat.

This time next year, you can build two houses in Jamaica.

VINCE *laughs*.

What's funny?

VINCE. I wish yuh all de luck / inna –

ROBERT. No, hold up a minute –

VINCE. Robert, yuh madda only jus gwan –

ROBERT. And I can't look after her any more but I can still look after you, Auntie Maggie –

VINCE. Me and Maggie live good. We alright –

ROBERT. Who's talking about being 'alright', I'm talking / about –

VINCE. Robert, yuh 'ear / whe me –

ROBERT. The Vince that grew me wasn't driving a Rover V8, cos he wanted to be 'alright'. We need to get clued up, Uncle V. It's not even about you, it's about Yvette, Yvette's children. Look how the Asian man's got it sorted. With what we spend in their shops, food and hair alone – we're feeding their families for generations to come. Well, what about us? I haven't been grafting since I was sixteen to just end up 'alright'. When you used to pick me up, Uncle V, the way those kids used to stare at us as we drove off. Those eyes still follow me wherever I go, whichever building I step into; only now they sit on the faces of grown men. They look at me same way, scratch their heads and wonder. The more they scratch the deeper I get under their skin. Let them feel us, Uncle V. Come in on it.

Beat.

VINCE. Yuh really wan lift up dis family, Robert?

ROBERT. Absolutely –

VINCE. Den yuh look after yuh sister dem. Lorraine, Trudy –

ROBERT. Trudy?

VINCE. See it deh –

ROBERT. This has nothing to do / with –

VINCE. A yuh sister –

ROBERT. I know who she is!

VINCE. Is because of yuh farda dat Trudy never reach England / and –

ROBERT. How was he gonna mind next man's baby, when he couldn't look after his own –

VINCE. It cut up Trudy inside, bad / bad, bad.

ROBERT. Mum always provided for Trudy. How many barrels did me and Lorraine watch travelling to Jamaica? Filled to the brim with things we couldn't touch –

VINCE. Yuh nuh how many times you madda beg yuh farda? –

ROBERT. Alvin!!

VINCE. She beg 'im fi send fi Trudy –

ROBERT. Uncle V, no disrespect, but, I'm trying to show you an opportunity. I don't want to discuss Alvin or Trudy right now –

VINCE. Yuh remember me friend from back 'ome?

ROBERT. What?

VINCE. Frank Thomas –

ROBERT. Who?

VINCE. We used to call him Tiger, because him love de solitary
life –

ROBERT. Uncle –

VINCE. When me first meet 'im, 'im 'ave whole heap a
property – Five house inna one street in Brixton. One night,
'im tek me to di pub, buy me a drink. / He must be ask about
ten man dat night what dem want. If a man seh 'beer', Tiger
buy 'im two, If a man seh 'rum', Tiger buy double. Tiger line
up alla de drinks dem, pon de table one by one like a domino
run. You tell me what 'im do next?

ROBERT. Uncle Vince –

I don't / know.

VINCE. Wham! 'Im box off all a di glass fi show, seh, 'im a big
money man. You tell me wheh Tiger end up now? –

ROBERT....

VINCE. In a nursing home. 'Im can't even hold 'im piss, much
less put it in a pot. Yuh can tek life fi sport, Robert. Burn all
yuh money in which ever way yuh want, but when yuh start
fi burn bridge – game done... Excuse me.

VINCE *exits upstage-left.*

ROBERT *stands alone for a beat.*

LORRAINE *enters in her nightclothes, holding a candle.*

They are in separate scenes and cannot see each other.

*Simultaneously they turn and face the picture of Gloria on
the wall.*

ROBERT *exits.*

LORRAINE *stands a moment longer.*

Lights change.

Into:

Scene Six

Night Five.

The middle of the night. LORRAINE *and* SOPHIE *are sitting cross-legged on the kitchen floor.*

SOPHIE *sits upright with her eyes closed.* LORRAINE *is fidgety with her eyes open. She tries to mirror* SOPHIE*'s position.*

SOPHIE. Inhale. Exhale. Slowly.

They breathe.

Again. Inhale. Exhale. Keep that going. Inhale. Exhale.

They breathe.

Inhale. Oh God. Oh, fuck. Fuck. / Fuck.

LORRAINE. What? What? What?

SOPHIE *cries.*

Did you feel something?

SOPHIE *cries.*

LORRAINE *looks up to the heavens.*

How the hell is that fair?

SOPHIE. I'm pregnant, Lorraine.

LORRAINE. What?

Beat.

You're forty-five.

SOPHIE. I know!

LORRAINE. Does Robert know?

SOPHIE *shakes her head.*

SOPHIE. No.

Scene Seven

Night Six.

VINCE *sits alone in the kitchen, drinking rum.*

Music is blaring from the other room. It's distinctly louder than previous nights.

We hear the start of 'Sugar Bum Bum' by Lord Kitchener. The guests show their appreciation, we hear 'Wheel and come again', 'Tune!', etc.

MAGGIE *enters from upstage-left.*

MAGGIE. Come on nuh, Vincent, a we tune dis.

VINCE. Nah sah, Maggie.

MAGGIE. W'appen to yuh? Yuh vex cos George bus yuh ass at dominoes?

　　VINCE kisses his teeth.

VINCE. Me tired, Maggie. Me tell yuh already.

MAGGIE. Is nuh tired yuh tired, is miserable yuh miserable.

VINCE. Is me always a complain bout me hip?

　　Beat.

MAGGIE. Is not me hip a give me complaint tonight, Vincent Armstrong.

　　VINCE gets up.

VINCE. Lard, Maggie, leave whe de argument.

　　He puts on his coat.

Mek we look fi go home.

　　VINCE exits upstage-right.

　　MAGGIE *refills* VINCE's *glass with more rum. She takes a mouthful and spits it out – deliberately allowing it to spray over the floor. She puts the glass down and looks up at Gloria.*

　　She exits, following VINCE.

Scene Eight

Two days later.

Day Eight.

LORRAINE, ANITA, ROBERT, MAGGIE *and* VINCE *around the kitchen table.* ANITA *has an iPad.*

LORRAINE. Okay. Are we all clear so far?

ANITA. Yep. Ten-thirty.

MAGGIE. Yuh nuh just seh eleven o'clock?

LORRAINE. Ten-thirty, if you're meeting us here. Eleven, if you're making your own way to the church.

VINCE. You book de horse and carriage?

ROBERT. Horse and carriage? Since when?

LORRAINE. I did mention it.

ROBERT. She was scared of horses.

LORRAINE. It was her wish, not mine.

MAGGIE. Gloria a go gallop to de gates of Jesus!

When I go, I want two white horses. And I want my coffin to shine like when Charlton Heston grin him teet.

VINCE. Yuh better tell yuh dawta dat. I will be long gawn.

LORRAINE. The service starts promptly at eleven. The church organist will play as Mum / enters the church.

MAGGIE. Mek sure yuh cook enough food fi tomorrow night.

LORRAINE. I'm sorry?

MAGGIE. Nine Night.

LORRAINE. We're not discussing the Nine right now, / Auntie Maggie.

MAGGIE. Lord, people travel all de way from Brixton last night and when dem reach – not even a dry piece of bread left fi dem fi scratch dem troat / wid –

LORRAINE. I didn't / know –

MAGGIE. Dat can't happen tomorrow evening. Mek sure.
Me already season me curry goat. Gloria spirit need plenty
feeding. Curry goat was she favourite.

ANITA. No it wasn't. She found it too bony.

MAGGIE. Maybe when you cook it – (*To* LORRAINE.) you
have any white candle?

LORRAINE.… ?

MAGGIE (*to* VINCE). Whe me tell yuh? Dem don't know whe
fi do. Remind me fi bring two white candle and a white
tablecloth.

ANITA. For what?

LORRAINE. Can we please get back to the service? What's
next, Anita?

ANITA. Pall-bearers.

LORRAINE. That's right. Robert's at the front. Winston and
Patrick are at the back. Uncle Vince, we wondered if you'd
like to be the pall-bearer next to Robert.

MAGGIE. Vince can't manage de coffin.

VINCE. Whe yuh a talk bout?

MAGGIE. 'Im legs long, but 'im arms too short.

VINCE. Tank you, Lorraine. Yes, I will.

ANITA. Readings.

LORRAINE. Anita's got the last reading, before I read the
eulogy –

ROBERT. Why's that?

LORRAINE. Why's what?

ROBERT. Why are you reading the eulogy?

MAGGIE. Exactly what I was tinking. Trudy should read it.
Trudy is de eldest.

LORRAINE. Yes, but Trudy's not going to be there.

ANITA. We could FaceTime?

ROBERT. Never mind Trudy, what about me?

ANITA. I'm serious –

LORRAINE. You?

ROBERT. Yes.

Beat.

LORRAINE. You didn't want to write it, so I didn't think you'd want to read it.

ROBERT. Did you ask?

Beat.

LORRAINE. Do you wanna read it?

ROBERT. Yeah. Yeah, I do as it goes.

LORRAINE. We're expecting a lot of people.

ROBERT. Yeah.

LORRAINE. It's a big church.

ROBERT. So?

LORRAINE. So, the words need to carry through to the back of the auditorium.

ROBERT. Just say what you're trying to say, Lorraine.

LORRAINE. You have a tendency to mumble.

ROBERT. What?

MAGGIE. Trudy / speak very clearly, and she 'ave a wonderful singing voice.

ROBERT. I don't mumble –

LORRAINE. Trudy's / not coming.

ROBERT. I make pitches to people all the time.

MAGGIE. She is coming.

LORRAINE (*to* ROBERT). It's not the same thing. (*To* MAGGIE.) No, she's not.

MAGGIE. I / speak wid ha last week.

ROBERT. I am gonna put one together actually.

LORRAINE. I spoke to her last night, and she hadn't even been to the Embassy.

MAGGIE. Suh?

LORRAINE. So, it wouldn't be possible to obtain a visa in time for the funeral next Thursday. We can't have two eulogies.

ROBERT. Who says we can't?

MAGGIE. What's de big rush anyway? Yuh can't wait?

ROBERT. Wait for what? Trudy's had ample time to sort out a visa.

MAGGIE. Yuh know how far she live from di Embassy?

ROBERT. So, how she gonna reach England, if she can't make the / forty miles to Kingston?

VINCE. I would like fi read someting.

MAGGIE. Dem road she haffi travel not easy-easy, yuh know.

LORRAINE. Finding a date that fits in with everyone's availability is, also, not easy-easy.

MAGGIE. Yuh hear dis, Vince?

LORRAINE. We also have to consider Mum. Every day that goes past, she's just lying there.

VINCE. A poem.

ANITA. Yeah, she wouldn't want that. It's really bad karma.

MAGGIE. Bad wha?

ANITA. Did anyone even ask her if she wanted to be buried?

LORRAINE. What?

ANITA. Because she was curious about cremation.

LORRAINE. Don't be / ridiculous, Anita.

MAGGIE. / A wha de?

ROBERT. Is she for real?

ANITA. She was. We discussed it. She read somewhere that cremations were better for the environment –

MAGGIE. We don't cook our people.

ANITA. You see? That's just ignorant –

MAGGIE. Whe yuh seh?

ANITA. You're gonna get nyam by maggots anyway.

ROBERT. Lorraine, I swear to God, speak to your daughter.

ANITA. She was very open to the idea.

LORRAINE. She's not being cremated, Anita. She's having a burial.

VINCE. I wouldn't mind it at all. Like de Indian Man. Burn de body, release de soul, ready to start over. A second chance.

Beat.

I want to read a poem at the service.

LORRAINE. A poem?

MAGGIE. What yuh know about poem?

LORRAINE. That would be lovely, Uncle Vince. What is it?

VINCE. Well...

MAGGIE. 'Im no know any poem.

LORRAINE. Have you got it with you?

VINCE. No.

MAGGIE. Wha me tell yuh?

LORRAINE. Do you know the title?

VINCE. No. Me a go write it.

LORRAINE. / Write it?

ANITA. A you dat, Uncle V?

LORRAINE. That sounds wonderful. Can I get back to you on
 that –

MAGGIE. Yes, Mr Shakespeare – gwan.

LORRAINE. I just need to check how we're doing for time,
 now that we're having two eulogies. What's next, Anita?

MAGGIE. Trudy! Me wan Trudy pon dis list.

LORRAINE. / Auntie Maggie –

ROBERT. Oh my God!

MAGGIE. Trudy is part of dis family. She clap eyes pon Gloria
 before oonuh even born. She have the right to see she madda
 before she end up inna de ground.

VINCE. Lard, Maggie. Yuh nuh hear wha dem seh? Dem can't
 leave Gloria coop up inna freezer like a damn fish. She need
 fi come off di cold ice and be lay to rest.

Silence.

MAGGIE. Well. Don't shoot de goose because di chicken never
 lay any egg.

ANITA. Do you mean – 'don't shoot the messenger'?

ROBERT*'s phone rings. He looks at it.*

LORRAINE. Can it wait? We're nearly finished.

He picks up.

ROBERT. Hello?

LORRAINE. Unbelievable.

ANITA. Do you want to move on to catering?

ROBERT. Speaking –

LORRAINE. No – that's taken care of.

ROBERT. Yeah, it's a good time… Just a minute…

ROBERT *gets up, exits downstage-left.*

(*Offstage.*) Go on…

VINCE. No Gloria fi cook de mannish water. Warm we up when we leave de graveside.

LORRAINE. Auntie Yvonne's going to do it.

MAGGIE. That woman gone senile. Yuh never 'ear wha she do at Pauline wedding? Season de chicken wid fish sauce. Blasted eediot.

Lorraine, yuh buy yuh madda stockings yet?

LORRAINE. Stockings?

MAGGIE. To put pon she foot. You need to get de nutmeg-coloured one. And she need a new wig. Dat one wheh she dead in look like any bird's nest. Yuh can't bury her in dat. She will frighten Jesus.

VINCE. Maggie.

MAGGIE. I'm meking sure she know what fi do.

Yuh want mi come wid you to dress her?

LORRAINE. No.

MAGGIE. Is not any and everybody know how fi do dem someting. Yuh remember Pinky? Is me dress her fa she funeral, yuh know?

Me grease up she foot good, help de stockings fi slide on. People tink, because yuh dead, yuh don't need Vaseline.

Yuh never 'ear people seh dem never see her a'look so good. Even she husband tek picture on WhatsApp to send back home.

LORRAINE. Right. That's it – meeting done.

MAGGIE. So quick?

LORRAINE *begins to gather their coats.*

LORRAINE. Yep – this one's yours, isn't it, Maggie?

MAGGIE. Why yuh always in a rush?

LORRAINE. I'm meeting the vicar in an hour. Anita'll drop you home.

ANITA. What?

LORRAINE. Mustn't keep a man of the cloth waiting.

LORRAINE *takes money out of her purse.*

Put that towards the petrol.

ANITA. Mum?

MAGGIE. But we never get time fi discuss de Nine –

LORRAINE. Don't you worry, Auntie Maggie, we'll have candles and tablecloths galore – you won't know if it's Nine Night or Hallowe'en.

MAGGIE. Hallowe'en?

VINCE. Come on, Maggie. Lorraine 'ave business fi attend to.

LORRAINE *bustles them out of the upstage-right door and exits.*

ANITA (*offstage*). Mum –

LORRAINE (*offstage*). Tell Rosa, Grandma's looking forward to seeing her tomorrow.

ROBERT *re-enters from downstage-left.*

MAGGIE (*offstage*). We can't mek it tonight. Yvette and Jonathan a tek us out fi dinner.

LORRAINE (*offstage*). Wonderful.

VINCE (*offstage*). See yuh tomorrow evening.

MAGGIE. Fi de Nine.

LORRAINE (*offstage*). Yes, Aunty Maggie. The Nine. See you then.

LORRAINE *re-enters.*

It's alright. You can go. The meeting's over.

LORRAINE pushes a chair in under the table. She allows herself to slump over it for a couple of beats.

She comes up.

Did you hear me?

She continues to push the chairs in.

ROBERT. I was being a dick. You do the eulogy.

LORRAINE ignores him. Goes to the fridge and takes out a bag of chicken wings.

I'll do that.

LORRAINE. What?

ROBERT. I'm at loose end this afternoon. Might as well help.

LORRAINE. Help? To season chicken?

ROBERT. I can cook, Lorraine.

LORRAINE. It's wings. They need plucking first.

ROBERT. I know how to prepare wings.

Beat.

She hands him the bag of wings.

LORRAINE. Alright.

ROBERT. You got any gloves?

LORRAINE. No. I use my hands.

ROBERT. Right.

He stands holding the bag awkwardly.

LORRAINE. I'll just carry on, shall I?

ROBERT. I normally use gloves.

LORRAINE takes back the bag of wings and starts preparing them.

ROBERT *watches her.*

I don't know how you're doing all this?

LORRAINE. Doing all what?

ROBERT. It's admirable, sis, but then you've always been like that. Busy. What was it Mum used to say? 'Lorraine come like bauxite. She inside everyting.'

LORRAINE *plucks.*

I keep thinking, any minute now, she's gonna appear at the bottom of the stairs. And give me that look. You know the one? Like if she hadn't seen me for a few days – dart me a frown before she'd crack a smile.

LORRAINE *plucks.*

I checked my phone today. To see if I had a missed call from her. Every lunchtime, the same conversation,

'Robert, yuh eat yet?'

'Whe Sophie cook fi yuh last night – yuh losing too much weight. Yuh nuh see how yuh neck string a stick out like marga turkey.'

LORRAINE. She called you every lunchtime?

ROBERT. One-thirty, on the dot.

LORRAINE.…

ROBERT. 'Nuh stretch yuh basket to whe yuh hand can't reach – '

LORRAINE. Why are you still here?

ROBERT. What?

LORRAINE. Normally, you can't get out the door fast enough.

ROBERT. I told you. I'm at a loose end…

Beat.

Everything's happening so fast.

LORRAINE.…

ROBERT. I need to talk to you, Lorraine.

Beat.

I know this guy. A property developer. He's interested in the house.

LORRAINE. Which house?

ROBERT. Come on, Lorraine –

LORRAINE. You're not serious?

ROBERT. He approached me –

LORRAINE. You bloody are / as well –

ROBERT. He's got several properties in the area –

LORRAINE. Robert, go home –

ROBERT. He'll pay properly –

LORRAINE. I'm not listening, / Robert –

ROBERT. We can get this done quite quickly –

LORRAINE. Have you no shame?

ROBERT. I'm not talking about selling tomorrow –

LORRAINE. She's still in here. Do you understand?

ROBERT. Where? Where is she? You keep saying that… I can't sleep in here like you do. It's not what she'd want –

LORRAINE. Don't talk to me about what my mum would want –

ROBERT. At some point, we've got to sell / the house –

LORRAINE. Don't you think I know that?

ROBERT. Property's gonna fall on its arse, this guy's / gonna –

LORRAINE. We're not having this conversation any / more –

ROBERT. We have to –

LORRAINE. This isn't property. This is her home. Our home. Three weeks ago she sat on that chair, laughing with Rosa and singing nursery rhymes, so don't / you dare –

ROBERT. She worked three jobs to keep this roof over our heads. And what? You wanna watch the value diminish, out of sentiment?

LORRAINE. Okay. You need to go now.

ROBERT. She's my mum too, Lorraine.

Beat.

LORRAINE. It was me that took voluntary redundancy to look after her. Every day for the last three-and-a-half months, I've been here, to hospital, to the chemist and back.

I can't talk about the house, Robert.

I can talk about anything else.

But not the house.

Not now.

Okay?

Beat.

So. Just go.

Beat.

Robert –

ROBERT. Thing is –

LORRAINE. If you really want to be helpful, fix the lock on the front door –

ROBERT. That was him / just now –

LORRAINE. I am so tired –

ROBERT. On the phone –

LORRAINE. So bloody / tired –

ROBERT. Lorraine –

LORRAINE. Yesterday, outside Sainsbury's, get this / there's this guy handing out vouchers for a free makeover –

ROBERT. Oh my God –

LORRAINE. – He takes one look at me, drops his gaze, waits
for me to walk past before he starts handing them out again. /
Can you believe that? –

ROBERT. I hate it when you do this.

LORRAINE. – His only task, all day, is to give those leaflets
out and he decided to hang on to one rather than waste it on
me. / I mean, I knew I looked rough, but – I've put more
thought into what Mum should look like next Thursday than
I have about myself. I bet you know what you're wearing?
Don't you?!

ROBERT. Tell you what? Let me know when you've finished.

I need money, Lorraine – okay?!

LORRAINE. Ha! Of course you do!

ROBERT. If we get in with this developer now, it works out
better for all of us.

LORRAINE. For you best. Come on then, why'd you need it?
What have you done?

ROBERT. What have I done? Don't ask me what I've done like
I'm some likkle eediot boy that arrived on the scene
yesterday. Better to ask me what I do, who I am? –

LORRAINE. Oh, get over yourself.

ROBERT. The genius that's gonna hit the rich list in five years'
time. That's who.

LORRAINE. Get on with it then. I'm not stopping you.

ROBERT. I can't!

LORRAINE. Why can't you?

ROBERT. Chris has fucked up! That's why he's not coming to
the funeral, Lorraine. He's fucked up and now he's gonna
walk away.

LORRAINE. He's fucked up how?

ROBERT. He's pissed off our main investor and now –

LORRAINE. What's that got to do with me?

ROBERT. How long is your redundancy gonna last? The
market's at its peak now, Lorraine. You need to stock up
every penny. When was last time you had to apply for a job?

Beat.

Let me take care of this now and in a year's time, you'll
thank me. We're just expediting the process. Trust me, take
a leap.

LORRAINE. That's where we differ. Even as kids. By nine
months, you'd mastered walking. Didn't matter how many
times you'd brock yourself up knocking into things, you'd
jump up and crash on, with Mum in awe. Whereas, with me,
she thought I was backward because I was nearly two before
I took my first steps. I don't leap, Robert. I don't enjoy the
feeling of falling.

ROBERT. You're not a kid now, Lorraine. You're a big grown
woman. A grandmother.

LORRAINE. Leave me alone, / Robert –

ROBERT. I've lost her too, Lorraine, I'm not losing any more,
do you understand me? I've lost her too, I'm not losing
any more…

Silence.

ROBERT *makes to leave.*

I'm bringing him round tomorrow afternoon –

LORRAINE. Sophie's pregnant!

ROBERT. What?

Beat.

What did you say?

Beat.

Lorraine?

Scene Nine

The next morning.

Day Nine – Nine Night.

LORRAINE *asleep on the sofa.*

A black woman, dressed in her Sunday best, watches over LORRAINE *as she sleeps.*

LORRAINE *stirs and opens her eyes.*

She sees the woman and screams.

TRUDY. Dat's nice. After me travel all dis way.

    Oonuh always leave yuh front door open?

Scene Ten

A few hours later.

LORRAINE, TRUDY, ANITA, MAGGIE *and* VINCE *in the kitchen.*

TRUDY *is in the middle of the sofa. From her suitcase she takes out gifts wrapped in newspaper and small black carrier bags.* VINCE *and* MAGGIE, *sit either side of her.*

TRUDY. Yam, plantain, dasheen, rum
    Green banana, Bami, nutmeg – rum
    Sweet potato, guinip – rum and chocolate tea
    Callaloo, Ackee and Mango from mi tree!

VINCE. / Lard, Trudy, yuh nuh easy!

MAGGIE. Lard, Trudy!

LORRAINE. We do have markets in England.

MAGGIE. Is stale food dat.

TRUDY. Cerasee fi yuh, Auntie Maggie.

MAGGIE. Yuh shouldn't worry yuhself, Trudy – Tank yuh.

ANITA. How did you even get all of that through customs?

TRUDY. Dem too busy a study Al Qaeda fi notice me – Uncle Vinnie.

She hands VINCE *a carrier bag.*

VINCE. Tank yuh, my dear.

TRUDY. Niecey.

She gives a bag to ANITA.

ANITA. Oh, thanks, Auntie Trudy.

TRUDY. Lorraine.

She hands one to LORRAINE.

LORRAINE. Thanks.

TRUDY. And one fi Niecey Junior.

VINCE *unwraps a bottle of white rum and some energy tonic drinks.*

VINCE. Yuh 'ave me just right, Trudy!

TRUDY. Nuh drink dem all at once.

ANITA *unwraps a green-and-yellow, two-piece, skirt and blouse. The tops have short frilly sleeves. The skirts are floor-length with frills at the bottom.*

ANITA. Wow – these are really cool.

TRUDY. Yuh like it?

ANITA. I love it!

TRUDY. Me ask Maggie fi guess oonuh size.

MAGGIE. It beautiful, Trudy.

VINCE. Is yuh mek it, Trudy?

TRUDY. How you mean? A me mek it, yes.

VINCE. Yuh business doing good?

TRUDY. Business booming.

LORRAINE. What is it supposed to be?

ANITA. Oh, my God! – Rosa's gonna look so cute. I'm putting mine on now.

ANITA *starts putting her outfit on on top of her clothes.*

TRUDY. Me mek one fi Yvette tuh. A tank yuh fi di discount pon me flight.

LORRAINE. Yvette got you a discount?

TRUDY. Yes, man.

LORRAINE. So when you said, you hadn't been to the Embassy?

TRUDY. Lie, me a tell! Me did wan surprise yuh.

MAGGIE. Yuh surprise me tuh. Me tink seh a next week yuh a come.

LORRAINE. You knew, all this time?

MAGGIE. Me tell yuh seh she a come.

TRUDY. Maggie!

LORRAINE. You knew too, Uncle Vince.

VINCE. Nah, dawta… Is really Trudy dis?

MAGGIE. A Trudy yes, inna England, to rass!

TRUDY *and* MAGGIE *have a long hug.*

LORRAINE *watches them.*

Gloria wouldn't believe she eye.

TRUDY. Me dream seh me seh ha, yuh know? De night she pass.

MAGGIE. Me tuh.

TRUDY. She was inna pure distress. She di try fi talk, but, when she open she mout, she speech drown inna water – a river gush from she tongue, like a waterfall, and wash she away.

LORRAINE. That doesn't sound like Mum at all. I never knew anything that could stop her from talking.

TRUDY. How she did look?

LORRAINE. Sorry?

TRUDY. Gloria. When she pass.

Slight beat.

ANITA. Peaceful.

TRUDY. Yuh believe seh is ten years since me last see ha.

Silence.

ANITA *walks to* TRUDY *and embraces her.*

ANITA. Sorry. It's just – You standing there – it's like – it's like she's here – you know? Your mannerisms, the way you laugh… everything…

TRUDY. Save yuh eye water, niecey. Gloria inna betta place. Tonight, yuh fi hold up yuh head in celebration, nuh bow it down wid contemplation – let me look pon yuh in yuh dress.

TRUDY *spins* ANITA *around.*

Yes, Miss Ting. Yuh shall go to de ball. – It really fit yuh. She really look like a Kumina dancer.

ANITA. A what dancer?

TRUDY. A dance from we village. Now yuh just fi learn how it go.

VINCE. Is more dan a dance. Is a way of life.

TRUDY. Dance troupe travel over Jamaica wid it now.

VINCE. Dem can dance it all dem like but is only de people weh grow inna it, know de real Kumina.

ANITA. Show us how it goes, Auntie Trudy.

TRUDY. Is fi Uncle Vinnie, fi show yuh.

VINCE. Me?

TRUDY. Yuh remember yuh and Gloria? At Granny funeral?

VINCE. Wha?

TRUDY. De two of yuh nearly set de place a blaze wid dem fiery move dem – Remember, Auntie Maggie?

MAGGIE. I wasn't at de funeral. I was at home. Sick. Wid a chest infection.

TRUDY. Show 'nita some move, Vinnie.

VINCE. Me – me – can't –

ANITA. Come on, Uncle Vince.

VINCE. Is not someting, yuh do just suh –

ANITA *takes out her phone.*

MAGGIE. Lef 'im. 'Im tired. 'Im bawling fi tired, all week.

TRUDY. Lorraine, yuh nah open fi yuh present.

LORRAINE. I'll open it later, thanks.

ANITA *is looking at a video on her phone.*

ANITA. Oh my God! Is this it – that's wicked!

TRUDY *joins* ANITA.

TRUDY. Yuh hear de drum dem? Bam, bam, bam, bam, bam, bam, bam, bam, bam!

She moves her hips in time with the drumming.

ANITA *copies her.*

ANITA. Wah, wah, / wah, wah, wah, / wah, wah, wah, wah…

TRUDY. Pick up yuh foot dem – Bam, bam, bam – Dat's it! Bwoy, likkle English can move!

They laugh.

ROBERT *and* SOPHIE *enter.*

ANITA *turns off the video.*

A beat.

ROBERT *and* TRUDY *face each other. A stand-off like a Western.*

TRUDY. W'appen? Yuh nah go greet yuh big sister? Or, yuh fraid fi touch black 'ooman? – Joke, me a joke.

ROBERT. Hello, Trudy.

TRUDY *embraces* ROBERT.

TRUDY. How yuh buff, suh? Dem must put someting sweet inna de Queen water.

She turns to SOPHIE.

A Stephy dis?

LORRAINE. / Sophie.

SOPHIE. Sophie. Lovely to meet you at last.

SOPHIE *puts out her hand.*

TRUDY. A wha dat?

TRUDY *embraces* SOPHIE.

Good to meet yuh tuh. Yuh sure yuh know how fi manage im?

SOPHIE. I'm sorry?

TRUDY *laughs.*

TRUDY. Yuh soon get used to me.

Slight beat.

LORRAINE. Drink, Sophie?

SOPHIE. I could murder a glass of water.

TRUDY. Try de cerasee, Auntie Maggie. It pick fresh from me back yard yesterday marning.

VINCE. Me can smell de sunshine from 'ere suh.

MAGGIE. A true – Lorraine, put on a pot of water.

LORRAINE. You're going to boil that now?

MAGGIE. Is dat a problem?

LORRAINE. No. Just usually takes a while for the smell to go, that's all.

MAGGIE. Suh open de window.

ROBERT looks at ANITA.

ROBERT. What are you wearing?

ANITA. Auntie Trudy made it.

SOPHIE. Oh, wow!

TRUDY. Me couldn't mek one fi yuh – Maggie never know yuh size.

MAGGIE. She put on weight –

SOPHIE. I'm working on my black woman's arse.

TRUDY. She 'ave humour. We a go get along jus' fine.

She takes out two bags.

She hands one to ROBERT.

Robert.

ROBERT. Ta.

She hands a bag to SOPHIE.

TRUDY. Dis fi yuh, Stephy.

SOPHIE. Sophie – Thank you.

ROBERT also has a bottle of rum.

ROBERT. Cheers.

SOPHIE unwraps a beautiful beaded necklace.

SOPHIE. Trudy, it's beautiful. Thank you so much.

TRUDY. A blind woman from me village mek it. Me glad yuh like it.

SOPHIE *goes over to* LORRAINE.

TRUDY *goes to* ANITA.

Me can't wait fi see Niecey Junior in she outfit tonight.

ANITA. Me neither.

ANITA *gets her phone to show pictures to* TRUDY.

ROBERT *sits near* VINCE.

LORRAINE. I'm so, so, sorry / I –

SOPHIE. He nearly crashed the car.

LORRAINE. What?

SOPHIE. I'm still shaking.

LORRAINE. What happened?

TRUDY. What a beautiful baby!

ANITA. Nathan's taken her swimming, but you'll meet them tonight.

SOPHIE. He went straight through a red light...

VINCE. Yuh look rough.

ROBERT. I didn't sleep too well, Uncle V.

LORRAINE. Sit down.

TRUDY. Dat's Nathan? 'Im look like Denzel – yuh nuh fool.

MAGGIE. Lorraine, yuh put on de water?

MAGGIE *makes her way over to* LORRAINE *and* SOPHIE.

ROBERT. How was your flight, Trudy?

TRUDY. Murder. Me did tink seh we a go drop outta de sky.

MAGGIE *puts the bag of cerasee down and starts looking through cupboards.*

ROBERT. It can be full-on, if you're not used to it.

TRUDY. Me mek dress fi private client in Miami and de Cayman Island. Me travel all de while.

LORRAINE. What are you looking for?

ROBERT. How long are you staying?

MAGGIE. Honey.

TRUDY. Me only just reach.

LORRAINE. There isn't any.

MAGGIE. Suh why yuh never seh dat inna de first place.

TRUDY. Come – Lorraine. Is what kinda celebration dis? – Bring some glass.

LORRAINE. What?

TRUDY. Mek we toast Gloria.

MAGGIE. And Trudy! Tank de Farda dat she reach safe!

TRUDY. Uncle Vince, tek a bokkle – open it. Lorraine, move quick nuh man.

LORRAINE. It's the middle of the afternoon.

TRUDY. A Nine Night dis.

LORRAINE *gets some glasses.* TRUDY *hands them out.* VINCE *opens a bottle of rum.*

TRUDY *takes the bottle and makes her way around the room, pouring.*

ANITA. Oh, a bit early for me, thanks.

TRUDY. Suit yuhself.

ROBERT. I'm in the car.

TRUDY. W'appen to yuh. A likkle can't touch a big man like yuh.

TRUDY *pours*.

MAGGIE. Splash likkle in me teacup, Trudy.

TRUDY *pours*.

Likkle more. Likkle more. Dat's it. Lorraine, stir de pot.

TRUDY. Yuh 'ave a glass, Sophie?

SOPHIE. I won't, thank you, Trudy.

TRUDY. Relax – 'im doing de driving.

SOPHIE. It's not that –

TRUDY. Yuh never taste rum till yuh taste dis –

ROBERT. She said no, alright?

TRUDY. W'appen? Yuh Christian?

SOPHIE. No, I'm not –

TRUDY. Yuh pon medication?

LORRAINE. / Trudy –

SOPHIE. No, it's –

TRUDY. Yuh pregnant?

SOPHIE. I...

Beat.

TRUDY. Me headside –

MAGGIE. Lard have mercy!

TRUDY. Lie, / yuh a tell!

VINCE. / A whe yuh a seh?

ANITA. You're shitting me.

MAGGIE. Me never tink me would live fi see de day!

ANITA. Don't be ridiculous. Sophie's not pregnant... Are you?

TRUDY. A double celebration to rass!!

VINCE. Robert! Yuh dark horse, yuh. Congratulations!

TRUDY *takes centre stage.*

TRUDY. Beg oonuh, tek up me hand.

She closes her eyes and holds out her hands.

MAGGIE. Come on, Vincent.

MAGGIE *joins* TRUDY, *followed by* VINCE. *They go either side of her.*

ANITA *then joins, next to* VINCE.

Oonuh. Come on.

SOPHIE *joins and takes* ANITA'*s hand.* ROBERT *rolls his eyes.* LORRAINE *reluctantly joins the other side of* SOPHIE. *They all look to* ROBERT *who closes the gap between* LORRAINE *and* MAGGIE.

TRUDY. Raise up oonuh hand!

Slowly, awkwardly, still holding hands, they raise their arms.

Praise de Lard, and de blessing of Jesus –

MAGGIE. Praise im –

TRUDY. Almighty Farda, surveyor of Heaven and Earth, we tank yuh fi dis day –

MAGGIE. We tank yuh, Lord –

TRUDY. Me reach in time fi share Robert and Sophie blessed news. Bright beginnings de bout –

MAGGIE. Fresh / beginnings –

TRUDY. – precious is de life of all of yuh children. Farda, shine yuh light pon Gloria –

MAGGIE. Shine it!

TRUDY. Protect ha. Cleanse and bathe ha.

MAGGIE. Bathe ha, Farda –

TRUDY. You alone is de sole creator. Wash away all she sin! / Amen.

MAGGIE. Amen!!

The sound of drums beating quietly begins. As it starts, apart from VINCE, *everyone else peels away.*

The drumming grows louder. VINCE *dances. He undoes his top two buttons as he moves. The drumming reaches a crescendo,* VINCE *keeps up with the beat. Suddenly the drumming stops.*

VINCE *stands still – into:*

Scene Eleven

Late on in the same evening.

VINCE. What is man,
    If not a visitor pon God's earth.
    Some come, enjoy dem stay,
    Others struggle fi find peace from day to day
    We all need precious help along the way.
    I had a precious friend in Gloria
    If I tap a rhythm
    She could fill the beat
    Me pulse run fast
    Like a cat pon –

TRUDY pops her head around the upstage-right door.

TRUDY. Yuh seen Auntie Maggie?

VINCE. No.

She exits upstage-right.

    Heat…
    Rest pon the other side, Gloria
    Me time soon come
    As me visit soon done

Greet me with that smile
And a likkle white rum.
Vincent.

LORRAINE *and* ANITA *enter from upstage-left.*

LORRAINE *is holding a bin liner.*

LORRAINE. They're waiting for you in the car, Anita.

ANITA. I'm just saying, it was a bit abrupt. People were in the flow, mid-tune –

LORRAINE. I promised next door we'd finish by midnight.

ANITA. She was having a grand old time –

LORRAINE. You've changed your tune.

ANITA. Cos I get it now, Mum. When the church ladies started praying, for that half an hour, I believed in God. Or, the hope that comes from having one. Someone looking out for Grandma. If someone's looking after her then she can still take care of us... And Auntie Trudy knocking out those rhythms with the dutchie lids, the room just transformed... I've felt so disjointed, Mum. You've always said: stay true to who you are, Anita. I'm trying. All who've been before and all who've yet to come were jamming in that room and making space for me... Did you see Rosa's eyes? Have you ever seen them look so bright?

LORRAINE. It's late, Anita. Take her home.

ANITA *gives* LORRAINE *a tight hug.*

ANITA. Night, Uncle V.

VINCE. Night, dawta.

ANITA *makes to go, stops and turns.*

ANITA. She was here tonight, Mum. She's happy.

She exits upstage-right.

LORRAINE *throws rubbish in the bin bag with vigour.*

VINCE. Nobody mean fi upset yuh, Lorraine.

LORRAINE. Who's upset? I'm not upset. I just want things put back where they were. – Where's Robert?

VINCE. We only did wan fi mek Gloria feel good.

LORRAINE. All day, all night; laughing, barging, eating, pissing – Every time I've tried to use the bloody bathroom someone's been in there. Enough is enough. I'm putting the cabinet back, calling you a cab, then I'm going to bed.

VINCE. Yuh can't move dat cabinet by yuhself.

LORRAINE. Wanna bet?…

LORRAINE exits upstage-left.

VINCE. Lorraine!

He follows after her.

On the heels of their exit, MAGGIE *comes through the upstage-right door, tentatively.*

MAGGIE. Psst…

TRUDY enters behind her.

Without speaking they begin to rearrange some of the furniture, occasionally stopping to check that no one is coming.

They are in agreement as to where things should go, but MAGGIE *takes the lead.*

When MAGGIE decides the room is ready, they stop.

Yuh ready?

TRUDY. Yeah man.

From offstage we hear ROBERT and SOPHIE's voices.

SOPHIE (*offstage*). All night, you've been avoiding me.

ROBERT (*offstage*). Now is not the time, Sophie.

SOPHIE (*offstage*). This has nothing to do with the business.

ROBERT (*offstage*). How can you say that?

SOPHIE (*offstage*). I couldn't care less.

MAGGIE indicates for TRUDY to pick up a bottle of rum left on the kitchen worktop.

They exit swiftly upstage-right.

SOPHIE and ROBERT enter from downstage-left.

I want this baby. Gloria wants this baby, did you not feel that tonight? I want it so much, you know what I did? I called my mother. This morning. I thought, fuck it. If I can tell her, I can tell anyone, and that'll make it real. And for all I know, she might say something nice. Something grandmotherly. Like Gloria would. She didn't. We exchanged a few words, then I hung up. Before the phone went down, do you know what she said? 'Goodbye, dear. Good luck with your caffè latte'... I thought that was quite witty, for her.

But that's it, isn't it? It's not the thought of becoming a father that scares you. It's the idea of having a child with me. Isn't it?

ROBERT. Nothing's changed for me, I made it really clear, from day one –

SOPHIE. The last time we set foot in my mother's house, the day you stood up for me – the expression on her face, I can see it now; I just remember thinking, 'My God, this man can do anything.'

ROBERT. Like an animal.

SOPHIE. What?

ROBERT. That's how your mum looked at me. If someone were to look at my child like that / it scares me what I might do to them. I don't think you do understand.

SOPHIE. I understand, Robert.

We hear:

LORRAINE (*offstage*). Oh God! Are you alright? Somebody help! Robert!... Robert!

VINCE (*offstage*). Lard, God...

LORRAINE (*offstage*). Can you stand up?

VINCE (*offstage*). Don't mek a fuss.

ROBERT *exits upstage-left.*

SOPHIE*, alone, looks up at Gloria*

ROBERT (*offstage*). I've got you, Uncle Vince.

LORRAINE (*offstage*). After three… / One, two, three.

ROBERT (*offstage*). One, two, three.

VINCE (*offstage*). Me alright, man.

ROBERT (*offstage*). Let me take him.

LORRAINE (*offstage*). Be careful.

SOPHIE *exits.*

ROBERT *and* LORRAINE *enter with* VINCE.

VINCE *is holding his back.*

VINCE. Me can manage.

LORRAINE. Let's put him on the – What's happened to the furniture?

ROBERT. Let's just put him down, Lorraine.

They sit VINCE *down.*

VINCE. God bless yuh.

ROBERT. What were you doing?

LORRAINE *looks around at the rearranged room.*

VINCE. Yuh sister seh, she wan fi move cabinet.

ROBERT. Not, the big one?

We hear a thump from upstairs.

They all look up.

What's that?

LORRAINE. Where's Trudy?

LORRAINE *exits upstage-right*.

ROBERT. Is it bad?

VINCE. Nah sah.

Slight beat.

Whe Sophie?

ROBERT. I think she might've gone, Uncle V.

A louder bang from upstairs.

We hear heated muffled voices of LORRAINE, TRUDY *and* MAGGIE.

What's going on?

LORRAINE (*offstage*). All now, you still can't answer the question.

TRUDY (*offstage*). Don't push her, Lorraine.

LORRAINE (*offstage*). I haven't touched her.

VINCE. Lard-'ave-mercy-in-heaven.

ROBERT *makes his way to the upstage-right door and is nearly trampled on as* TRUDY, MAGGIE *and* LORRAINE *come charging through.*

MAGGIE (*offstage*). Yuh wan me brok me neck?

TRUDY (*offstage*). Tek time, Auntie Maggie.

LORRAINE (*offstage*). Who said you could go in there?

TRUDY (*offstage*). Yuh tink seh yuh a de boss?

LORRAINE (*offstage*). Sneaking around de place like a damn teef.

LORRAINE *slams the door shut behind them.*

TRUDY. Is who yuh a call teef?!

MAGGIE. Outta order, she outta order.

VINCE. What's going on, Maggie? / Aigh…

TRUDY. A who wan fi teef any of dis ole brock?

ROBERT. Lorraine – ?

LORRAINE. I caught / the two of them up there –

TRUDY. / Catch what?

MAGGIE. Yuh 'ear she?

LORRAINE. Searching up the place –

ROBERT. What did I tell you?

LORRAINE. Caught red-handed. / Well, you're not leaving until –

TRUDY. / Seh yuh catch me more one more time and see if yuh can catch yuh teet when I box out every last one a dem from yuh mout?

MAGGIE. Jesus Christ!

LORRAINE. Come nuh!

VINCE. Oonuh stop it and calm down… (*Holding his back.*) Lard.

MAGGIE. Lorraine, apologise.

LORRAINE. Apologise for what!

MAGGIE. Yuh already mash up tonight proceedings wid yuh feisty self.

ROBERT. Why are you in cahoots with her, Auntie Maggie?

TRUDY *kisses her teeth*.

LORRAINE. What have you taken?

VINCE. Is not teefing dem teefing.

MAGGIE. Oonuh is just pickney to me. Me nuh answerable tuh any pickney.

LORRAINE. Alright then, you can answer to the police –

LORRAINE *moves from the door to find her phone.*

TRUDY. Yes! Yuh call dem!

VINCE. Yuh haffi explain yuhself, Maggie –

MAGGIE. Shut yuh mout. She lucky me lef ha standing after she a bawl out teef.

ROBERT. Explain what –

LORRAINE. Everything you've asked me to do tonight, I've done it. Put up with your, 'In Jamaica "we do it like this". In Jamaica "we don't do it like that".' Well, this isn't Jamaica – this is my mother's home, and all I've asked is that you respect it. I've let people in here, tonight, friends of yours that look like candidates for death row –

TRUDY. Yuh stuck-up –

LORRAINE. I told you to stay out of her room. / It still smells of her in there. I haven't even changed her sheets. Everything in there was exactly where she left it. It's not just about her stuff. It's a mapping of her routine. The dictionary under the Bible. The slippers next to the chest, that's where she left them. And, you two descend in there, like jankcrows –

ROBERT. You were in her room?

TRUDY. Is who yuh a call jankcrow? When is yuh a circle round Gloria like seh is only yuh a suffer –

MAGGIE. Of all of Gloria pickney, Trudy is de only one wid de intelligence fi know wha fi do. Is Gloria last night in she yard. A spirit never wan fi leave de family home. You have fi encourage dem out, disorientate dem, put dem mattress up against de bedroom door – if Gloria get trap inna dis house tonight – oonuh will fart!

ROBERT. What the hell are you talking about?

LORRAINE. Get them out, Robert. I swear to God –

MAGGIE. Mi nah leave dis yard before I see Gloria pass through wid me own two eye.

VINCE. Oonuh stop de argument. Gloria need fi mek she journey in peace. Travel back to Africa.

MAGGIE. Is Jamaica she come from, yuh blasted eediot.

LORRAINE. Get out. I'll call the police, I swear to God – Watch me get your arse deported!

TRUDY. Yuh can call de ratiid Queen, fi all I business. Who wan fi stay inna dis yard? Dis yard a suck out me blood! Gloria still inna it. The same pussy whe yuh spring from, is de same pussy whe trap me –

ROBERT. What did you say?

MAGGIE. Tek it easy, Trudy.

TRUDY. Yuh know weh it feel like, when de hole inna yuh heart carve out by yuh own mudda? Is like I spend my whole life stuck inside dat woman. Can hear she voice, but can't see, feel, touch. Is not botheration me a look. Is liberation. Liberation from de fuckeration, so I can draw breath, and fly free!

VINCE. Me beg yuh fi stop dis, Trudy.

TRUDY. Me was four years old when she look me dead inna de eye and tell me seh she a go to Ingland pon holiday –

ROBERT. Same old shit –

TRUDY. And me seh, 'But, Mummy, Ingland nuh freezing cold?'

LORRAINE. What do you think would have happened if she had brought you with her? She came with nothing –

TRUDY. See Auntie Maggie deh. Ask ha if she would abandon she own pickney.

LORRAINE. She wanted to build a better life –

TRUDY. A better life fi sheself!

LORRAINE. That's not true.

ROBERT. She wrote to you every month –

LORRAINE. Clothed and fed all of us, same way.

TRUDY. Year after year, mi long fi Mummy fi come back home. Finally, she reach. But, wid she two new pickney. Yuh remember? Granny seh, 'Suprise, Trudy! Meet yuh brudda and sista.' Oonuh look at me, coop up inna hell. Soak up de heat before you fuck off to your paradise.

ROBERT. You were the one she saved.

LORRAINE. We all had it hard, Trudy, but there wasn't a day, not one day, that she wasn't thinking of you. I know and he knows because we were here. Every year, September 12th, she'd wake us up to perform your birthday ritual. Do you remember, Robert? She'd make an enormous sponge cake, that we couldn't eat until bedtime, to fit in with the time difference, when you got home from school. And she'd take out the tablecloth –

ROBERT. That's right.

LORRAINE. That only came out / at Christmas.

ROBERT. Christmas Day.

LORRAINE . And we'd stand round the table and sing. Not 'Happy Birthday', cos that was too upbeat. – She'd make us stand with our hands clasped in the prayer position and sing, 'How Great Thou Art', as though you were God. She worshipped you.

TRUDY. September 13th.

LORRAINE. What?

TRUDY. Mi birthday is September 13th. Not the 12th. And me fucking hate sponge cake.

LORRAINE. She did the best she could.

TRUDY. She left me behind. She forsake me, like God forsake Jesus.

LORRAINE. Except you weren't pinned naked to a cross, were you?

Who was it that gave you the money to set up your dressmaking business in the first place?

ROBERT. Tell her!

TRUDY. Everyting for oonuh in Ingland is money, innit? Fuck up people life, and tink seh yuh Sterling can fix it.

LORRAINE. You didn't refuse it though, did you? Like you refused her. What about when you're flying off to Miami and the Caymen Islands –

ROBERT. That's right.

LORRAINE. Still feel abandoned then? –

VINCE. Dis is not how fi do it, children –

MAGGIE. Lef dem, Vincent –

ROBERT. She started dis, Uncle V –

TRUDY. Yes! And after de funeral me a go mek sure it done!

ROBERT. Really? So how much is it gonna take then, Trudy?

ROBERT *takes his wallet out.*

He starts to throw money out on the floor.

Let's cut the bull. How much? / So we can stop the pretence –

MAGGIE. / Damn disgrace –

VINCE. Gloria heart a bleed!

LORRAINE. This isn't about money, Robert. Look at her. I know exactly what she wants. But I don't know what she's going to do with it. All that bitterness, blistering inside of you. You sent her from this life to the next carrying shame. You can't do any more. She was sick for months. Where were you? She asked me over and over again, 'Trudy call?' 'Trudy coming?' I've always been rubbish at lying, but, my God, I got good at it by the end. Have you ever seen disappointment on a dying face? It's not like she didn't try and make it up to you. When Alvin left. She sent for you. Finally, she could have the family she'd always wanted. She called you up. Begged you to come. Didn't she? What? Can't you remember? We do – don't we, Robert? She left us in the house and went to find a phone box. She was gone for ages, I started to get worried. I went into my room and started moving things around, thinking about where you would sleep. As though you were going to walk through the door with her. I didn't even mind sharing her, we were used to that. Half of her was always tied up with you. When she got back in, she didn't look at me. I didn't know how you'd said it but it was clear. 'Trudy not coming.' You were right not to come. Mum wanted you but England didn't. It didn't want her. It didn't want them. It didn't want him. It didn't want me. So, you can stand there, victorious, watch the rest of us grieve / but, I know –

TRUDY. When did she send fi me?

LORRAINE. What?

TRUDY. Name the day. The year, the hour, the second dat she send / for me.

LORRAINE. I remember it well, I was twelve –

TRUDY. She never!

LORRAINE. Yes, she did!

TRUDY. See Vince and Maggie a siddown deh. Yuh ask dem when yuh mudda ever send fi me. Never, never, never, never, never, never, ever, never, never!

LORRAINE. You're a liar!

TRUDY. Ask dem.

ROBERT. You choose to stay with your granny –

LORRAINE. Uncle Vince?

Slight beat.

Auntie Maggie?

Slight beat.

Answer me!

VINCE. I never hear of dat, Lorraine.

TRUDY. Fi oonuh madda was de liar. Not me. Me nuh business bout fi oonuh money. Every part of me, whe yuh see a stand up in front of yuh, well a Jamaica it mek. England nuh 'ave nuttin fi do wid it.

Mi come a Ingland fi bury de woman dat born mi. Mi grieve for me mudda already, de day mi granny dead.

Silence.

MAGGIE (*sings*). Precious Lord, Take my hand,
Lead me on, let me stand
I'm tired, I'm weak, I'm lone,
Through the storm, through the night,
Lead me on to the light,
Take my hand, Precious Lord, Lead me home
When my way –

MAGGIE *freezes. Stares out front.*

VINCE. Maggie?

Slight beat.

Maggie?

ROBERT. What's she looking at?

VINCE. Maggie?

TRUDY. Myal.

ROBERT. Uncle V?

MAGGIE. Gloria… Yuh reach.

ROBERT. Nah, nah, nah, not at all – fuck this –

MAGGIE. What a whe yuh look good, Gloria – Dead really suit yuh.

ROBERT. Uncle V, make her stop.

VINCE. Yuh can see ha good, Maggie?

ROBERT. This isn't funny –

TRUDY. Granny wid ha, Maggie?

ROBERT. That's enough. Lorraine – I'm gone!

ROBERT *turns to go.*

MAGGIE. Robert. Yuh madda seh she want fi see you.

Wherever ROBERT *has got to, he stops dead in his tracks, facing the door upstage-left. His back to* MAGGIE.

He buries his face in his hands.

ROBERT. Listen, Auntie Maggie –

MAGGIE. Move yuh hands from yuh face. She want fi see yuh good-good.

LORRAINE *and* VINCE *watch* ROBERT *as he slowly drops his hands, his back still facing* MAGGIE, MAGGIE*'s back facing his.*

Turn around.

ROBERT *doesn't move.*

Never turn your back pon a spirit.

ROBERT *reluctantly turns around.*

ROBERT. So. Now what?

MAGGIE*'s body bends and bolts.*

LORRAINE. Oh, my God.

When MAGGIE *speaks her voice is deeper.*

MAGGIE/GLORIA. Robert – When Crow look down from the mountain top / him see plenty food, but him wound him wing, so him 'fraid fi tek de chance. Him look up to de sky. Eagle a come. Crow seh, 'Eagle, beg yuh give me a chance. In a few hours I will surely be dead. Eat me if you must, but leave it till de mornin'. Mek me have one last meal.' Eagle lick im beak, and nyam Crow same way and seh, 'Crow, yuh shudda tek de chance when yuh did have it.'

LORRAINE. Mum?

MAGGIE/GLORIA. Trudy?

Mi leave off de heavy load me affi carry inna dis life. Every step mi tek forward, mi balance wid de step mi lef behind.

One can't exist without de udda. Freedom have a rising motion. She stretch out she hand and invite every single one'a we. Latch on, but yuh haffi unclench yu fist.

Lorraine?

LORRAINE. Yes. I'm here, Mum.

MAGGIE/GLORIA. Lorraine, yuh – yuh –

MAGGIE*'s body jolts. She doubles over. She speaks as though she's in pain.*

Gloria, yuh need to pass now.

LORRAINE. What? No. Wait. She can't –

MAGGIE. Somebody open the door.

VINCE. Lorraine –

LORRAINE. No. She hasn't finished –

MAGGIE. Move from de path.

LORRAINE. No. Mum. Wait –

MAGGIE. Trudy, open it –

MAGGIE *groans.*

TRUDY *makes for the door.* LORRAINE *runs at* TRUDY *and pulls her down to the floor.*

LORRAINE. Leave it. Let her speak. What were you going to say, Mum?

TRUDY. Come offa me.

ROBERT. Lorraine. What the fuck are you doing?

LORRAINE *holds* TRUDY *down.*

VINCE *tries to get up but his back gives out.*

VINCE. Let her go, Lorraine!

ROBERT *stands, watches the chaos around him.*

LORRAINE *still has hold of* TRUDY.

LORRAINE. It's okay. You can speak to me now. Mum. I'm here. You can speak to me.

VINCE. Robert, get her off before she kill her.

MAGGIE *continues to groan*.

ROBERT *pulls* LORRAINE *off* TRUDY.

ROBERT. Get off her, Lorraine. Stop!

TRUDY *is on all fours, gasping for breath*.

MAGGIE. Pass, Gloria.

ROBERT. Shut up, Maggie!

MAGGIE. Open the door.

MAGGIE *begins to chant*.

TRUDY *crawls towards the door*.

ROBERT. Stop this now, Maggie.

VINCE. Gloria a go get trap in ya!

LORRAINE *runs to the kitchen drawer, pulls out a knife and holds it towards* TRUDY.

LORRAINE. I said, leave the fucking door alone.

ROBERT. / Lorraine!!

VINCE. Lard, Gad, Lorraine, put dat down!

LORRAINE. No! She needs to speak. Let her speak.

TRUDY *backs away from the door*.

MAGGIE *stops chanting and slumps on the chair exhausted*.

Mum? I'm here. What?

What is it?

I'm here now.

What do you need?

I'm here.

Have I done everything?

Do you like your dress?

I couldn't decide between the purple or cream.

Has the pain stopped now?

I said you were losing weight.

'Mi fine' you said.

You're not, Mum.

You're not.

We waited at the hospital –

'Whe dem seh?' You said. 'It a go kill mi?'

'I don't know, Mum. It might – I don't – I – Yes, yes, yes, It's going to kill you.'

'Me?' You said.

'Don't look so scared. I'll hold your hand. I'll rub your back.'

You faded so fast.

'The soup too hot.' You said, 'Mek it cool.'

I combed your hair.

'De room too hot,' you said, 'Open de window.'

I changed your sheets.

'Me foot feel heavy,' you said,

I massaged your feet.

I pulled up your blanket.

I notice you smile.

I notice you breathe.

'Mum?' I said.

'Mum?'

Yuh squeezed my hand.

Mum?

Mum?

Mummy??

Silence.

ROBERT. The knife, Lorraine?

Beat.

Lorraine?

LORRAINE *walks towards the door, the knife still in her hand.*

LORRAINE *stands in front of the door. She opens it.*

TRUDY *exhales.*

LORRAINE. She's gone.

LORRAINE *crumples to the floor and sobs.*

MAGGIE *begins to cry.*

ROBERT *watches on.*

VINCE. Gawn? She really gawn, Maggie?

MAGGIE. You tell me, Vincent Armstrong. You tell me.

ROBERT *goes to* LORRAINE.

Takes the knife out of her hand.

They hold each other.

Blackout.

The End.

'A great published script makes you understand what the play is, at its heart' *Slate Magazine*

Enjoyed this book? Choose from hundreds more classic and contemporary plays from Nick Hern Books, the UK's leading independent theatre publisher.

Our full range is available to browse online now, including:

Award-winning plays from leading contemporary dramatists, including *King Charles III* by Mike Bartlett, *Anne Boleyn* by Howard Brenton, *Jerusalem* by Jez Butterworth, *A Breakfast of Eels* by Robert Holman, *Chimerica* by Lucy Kirkwood, *The Night Alive* by Conor McPherson, *The James Plays* by Rona Munro, *Nell Gwynn* by Jessica Swale, and many more…

Ground-breaking drama from the most exciting up-and-coming playwrights, including Vivienne Franzmann, James Fritz, Natasha Gordon, Ella Hickson, Anna Jordan, Jack Thorne, Phoebe Waller-Bridge, Tom Wells, and many more…

Twentieth-century classics, including *Cloud Nine* by Caryl Churchill, *Death and the Maiden* by Ariel Dorfman, *Pentecost* by David Edgar, *Angels in America* by Tony Kushner, *Long Day's Journey into Night* by Eugene O'Neill, *The Deep Blue Sea* by Terence Rattigan, *Machinal* by Sophie Treadwell, and many more…

Timeless masterpieces from playwrights throughout the ages, including Anton Chekhov, Euripides, Henrik Ibsen, Federico García Lorca, Christopher Marlowe, Molière, William Shakespeare, Richard Brinsley Sheridan, Oscar Wilde, and many more…

Every playscript is a world waiting to be explored. Find yours at **www.nickhernbooks.co.uk** – you'll receive a 20% discount, plus free UK postage & packaging for orders over £30.

'Publishing plays gives permanent form to an evanescent art, and allows many more people to have some kind of experience of a play than could ever see it in the theatre' *Nick Hern, publisher*

www.nickhernbooks.co.uk